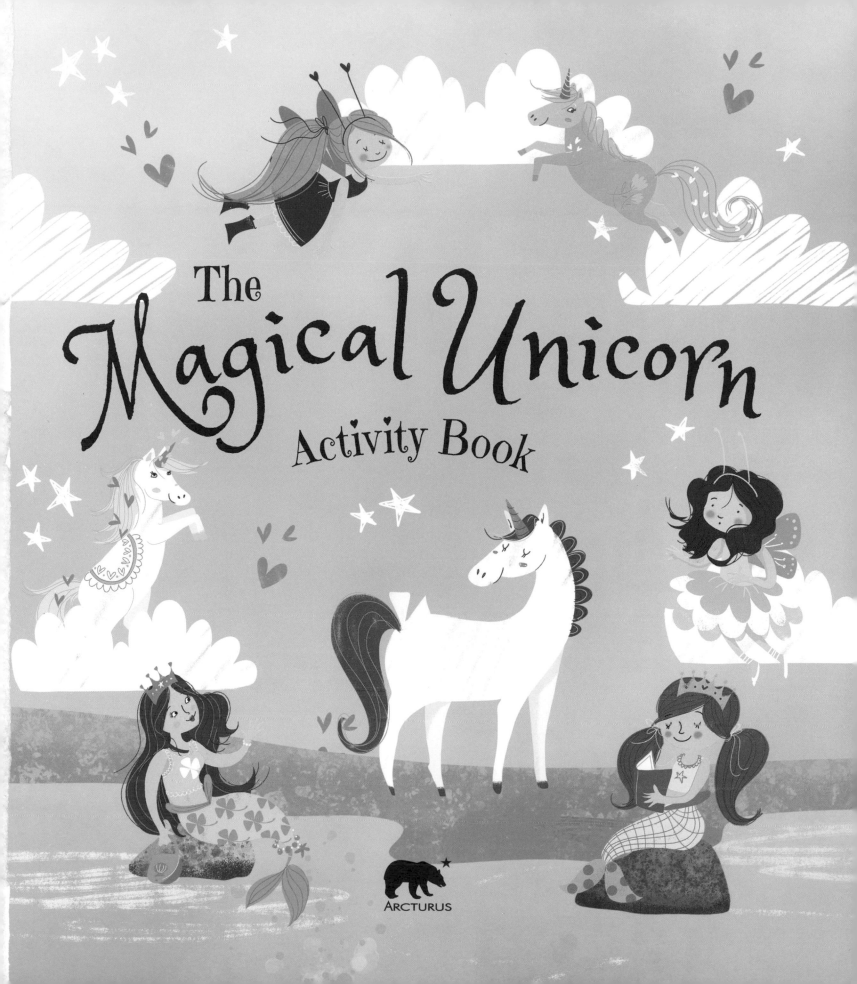

The Magical Unicorn
Activity Book

ARCTURUS

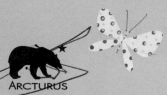

This edition published in 2018 by Arcturus Publishing Limited
26/27 Bickels Yard, 151–153 Bermondsey Street,
London SE1 3HA

Illustrated by Samantha Loman
Written by Samantha Williams and Lisa Regan
Edited by Susannah Bailey
Designed by Well Nice Ltd and Trudi Webb

ISBN: 978-1-78950-090-5
CH006978NT
Supplier 29 Date 1018 Print run 7884

Printed in China

Come On In!

Welcome to this magical land, where unicorns roam, fairies fly high, and mermaids splash in a pink lemonade sea. But which pathway leads to the castle? Is it A, B, or C?

Twin Teaser

These unicorns are frolicking in the magical meadow.
But can you tell which two are twins?

Time for Tea!

The furry pet friends are having a picnic. Can you complete the scene by filling in the missing pieces?

1

2

3

4

5

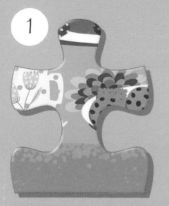

Under the Sea

Welcome to the mermaids' watery world!
Can you spot the items shown below?

Beautiful Babies

These playful dolphins are returning to their mothers. Can you follow the lines to pair them back up?

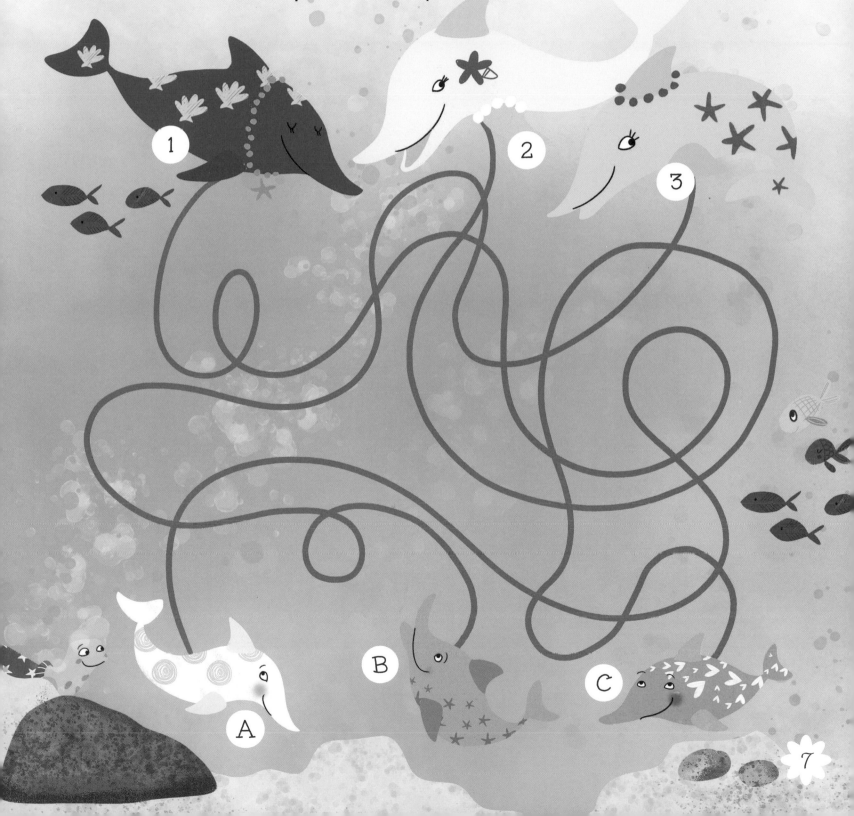

Party Prep

Springblossom loves getting dressed up!
Which of these silhouettes is an exact match for her?

#selfie

These unicorn friends have been taking photos, but one looks slightly different. Can you figure out which one?

Gift Giving

Aqua is making a necklace for her friend, Pearl. Study the pattern, and work out which two shells she needs to thread onto the end.

Party Time

Bring this underwater party to life with lots of blues, greens, and pretty pinks.

Super Starfish

Sunshine is searching for her special starfish, which has six points, but it has become mixed up with the starfish that have five points. Can you find it?

Friendly Fish

Can you find a way for Misty the mermaid to swim through the sea? She can only follow the fish that look like this. →
She can swim up, down, left, and right, but not diagonally.

Start

Finish

Who's Your Unicorn Best Friend?

Answer the questions and follow the arrows to find out!

START

Sleepover or skate party?

Jogging or swimming?

Glitter or grunge?

Lie-in or up and about?

TV or talking?

Spots or stripes?

Ponytail or let it loose?

Dolphins or sharks?

Singing or Dancing?

Gold or silver?

Stars or the Moon?

Reading or gaming?

Smoothie or Milkshake?

Your friend is Astra. Her name means "Shining Star."

Your friend is Aurora. Her name means "True Dawn."

Your friend is Flora. Her name means "Pretty Flower."

Stormy Seas

Take a look at these two pictures, and try to spot eight differences between them.

15

Find Me!

The baby unicorns are playing hide-and-seek!
Can you spot all seven of them?

Best Fairy Friends

Which fairy doesn't have a BFF in a matching outfit?

17

Bobbing Along

Match these cute seahorses into pairs. Which seahorse doesn't have one?

Secret Message

Fill in all the boxes that contain the letters S, E, and A.
The remaining letters spell a message from Coral and Shelly.

E	S	A	S	S	A	E	E	S	A
A	E	S	E	E	S	E	A	A	E
S	E	S	J	E	O	A	I	E	N
A	E	E	E	S	A	S	E	A	S
E	S	O	S	U	E	R	S	A	S
A	E	A	E	A	S	A	S	E	E
E	S	E	E	S	A	S	A	E	S
S	A	S	F	A	U	A	N	A	E
S	S	E	A	S	A	S	E	A	S
E	E	A	S	A	A	E	A	S	A

Unique-orn

Carefully copy this picture of Flowerpuff using the grid below to help you.

20

Which Way?

Can you help Blossom find the path back to the pink palace?

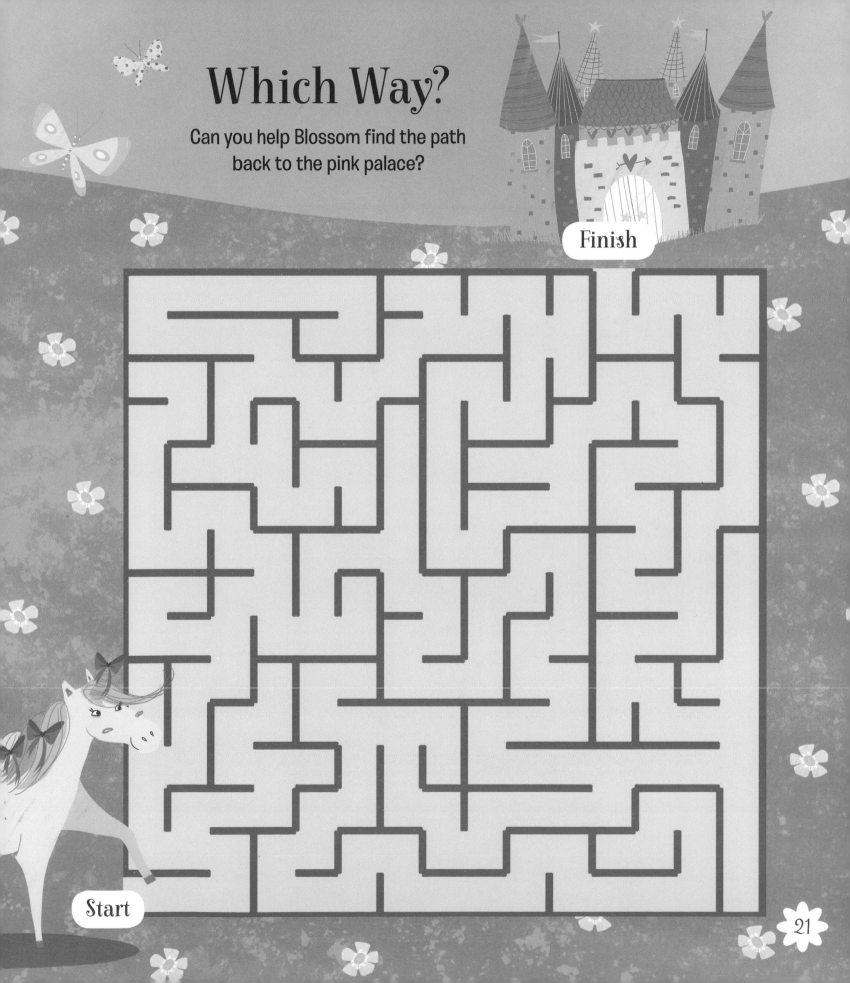

Finish

Start

Seeing Stars

The mermaids are star-hunting in this shipwreck scene.
How many are there? Remember to look for all types of star!

Winged Wonders

Are there more fluttering fairies or beautiful butterflies in this scene?

Magical Trail

Can you find all these magical words in the grid below? Words are spelled out forward, backward, and diagonally.

MERMAID   UNICORN   SHIMMER   FAIRY
SPARKLE   WAND   RAINBOW   WINGS

M	E	R	W	I	N	R	G	H	W
E	U	S	P	A	R	K	L	E	I
D	S	N	D	R	W	I	N	G	S
I	F	A	I	R	Y	D	A	I	R
A	A	W	U	C	W	A	N	B	A
M	E	N	N	S	O	B	O	A	I
R	I	N	I	H	W	R	D	S	W
E	S	R	C	F	A	I	N	H	W
M	P	R	E	M	M	I	H	S	A
A	R	A	I	N	B	O	W	I	N

25

Round and Round

Find out what this octopus is called by circling every other letter from left to right, starting at the top. These letters spell her name. The first one has been done for you.

S _ _ _ _ _ _

Coco the Clown

Coco is another of the mermaids' friends. He looks a lot like the other clownfish, but not exactly the same. Where is he?

Pool Party!

Which inflatable flamingo float looks different from the rest? And which watermelon float has a different number of seeds?

Dreamy Design

Draw your perfect palace in the magic mirror, and
then use your pens and pencils to bring it to life.

Magical Mer-king

Which of the jigsaw pieces below completes the royal scene?

A B C D

Undersea Creatures

Can you find these swimming sea creatures hidden in the grid?
Words can be found forward, backward, and diagonally.

CRAB

OCTOPUS

FISH

DOLPHIN

S	E	A	N	O	I	L	A	E	S
S	D	O	L	P	H	I	N	S	F
H	E	W	E	R	P	N	C	R	I
E	C	A	T	H	C	A	E	C	S
L	A	R	H	P	R	B	A	U	H
A	B	S	A	O	T	E	U	C	B
H	S	O	L	B	R	L	S	O	O
W	R	P	L	O	B	S	T	E	R
P	R	T	S	W	L	S	E	P	O
S	U	P	O	T	C	O	T	S	B

SEAHORSE

WHALE

SEALION

LOBSTER

31

Shiny Crown

Milly the unicorn will crown one of these fairies queen for the day, but which one? Solve the clues to find out.

1. Her hair is braided.

2. She has a heart-shaped wand.

3. She is not wearing ballet shoes.

4. She isn't wearing a belt.

Cloud Kingdom

Can you discover eight differences between these two floating fairy castles?

Golden Bells and Pearl Shells

Welcome to the royal palace! How many golden bells and pearl shells can you count in this picture?

BELL

SHELL

34

Beautiful Bows

Which unicorn is wearing each pretty patterned bow?
Follow their twisting tails to find out!

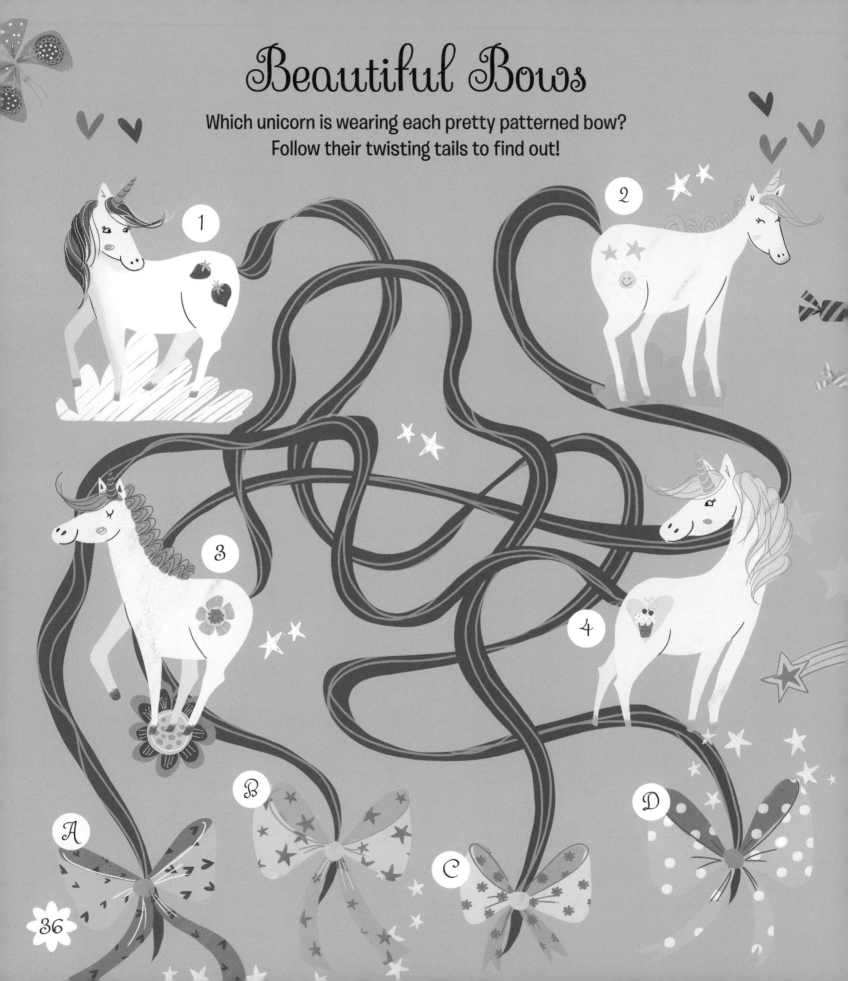

Pearl Problem

The mermaids are collecting pearls. Solve the equations on their bags to find out which mermaid has collected the most.

5×3

$15 + 4$

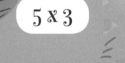

8×2

$25 - 4$

$16 + 4$

Wavy Hair!

Pearl is washing her beautiful, long curls. Which of her shadows exactly matches the main picture?

A

B

C

D

Mer-maze

Can you help Coral avoid the eels on her way back to the palace?

39

Draw Me!

Follow the steps to create your own magical unicorn.

Queen of the Arts

The Fairy Queen loves being creative.
She has painted six unicorn pictures that look identical.
Can you tell which is the odd one out?

Shell Sorting

Sort these special, magic shells into groups that are the same.
Which type are there most of? Which is the smallest group?

Home Sweet Home

Copy this picture of the underwater palace, and then decorate it with your pens or crayons.

Lost Jewels

The Unicorn Queen has lost her beautiful necklace! Can you help her find it? She needs to search her stones in a particular order, going up, down, right, and left, but not diagonally.

1

2

3

Start

Finish

Magical Memories

Look at this picture for two minutes. Then, turn the page, and answer the questions without looking back.

Magical Memories

1. What is the pink unicorn holding?

....

2. Is one mermaid wearing a crown or a hat on her head?

....

3. How many fairies are there?

....

4. How many unicorns have bows on their tails?

....

5. How many mermaids are there?

....

6. What is sitting on top of the toadstool?

....

Missing Link

Cross out any letter that appears twice. The leftover letters spell the name of a shelled sea creature. Which one is it?

A P L W

O W B F

S T F P

E R A

Shining Bright

Can you find this line of four jewels somewhere in the large pattern?

Find the Fairy

The fairies are playing hide-and-seek with the unicorns
and have hidden among the flowers.
Can you spot all ten of them?

Lost and Found

Which of the treasure chests is the one the prince is looking for? Use the clues to work it out.

It has a lock on it.

It has a flat lid.

It has handles.

It contains a golden goblet.

A

B

C

D

E

F

50

Watery Words

How many smaller words can you make, using the letters from HIDDEN TREASURE?
Write them down as you think of them.

HIDDEN TREASURE

Magical Unicorn Name

Your birth month + your fave baby animal = your unicorn name!
For example, if you were born in April and liked kittens, your name
would be Golden Starlight. Write down yours below!

JANUARY	SPARKLY	JULY	SHINY
FEBRUARY	DIAMOND	AUGUST	RAINBOW
MARCH	CRYSTAL	SEPTEMBER	DREAMY
APRIL	GOLDEN	OCTOBER	TWIRLY
MAY	GLITTERY	NOVEMBER	CANDY
JUNE	TWINKLY	DECEMBER	SHIMMERY

PUPPY	SUNSHINE
KITTEN	STARLIGHT
DUCKLING	SUNFLOWER
LAMB	BUTTERCUP
PIGLET	PRINCESS
BUNNY	MOONBEAM
CHICK	FIRE GLOW

My unicorn name is:

....

My friend's unicorn name is:

....

52

Adorable Outfits

The fashion fairies are sorting out their clothes, but everything is now out of place. Can you help put everything back together?

Wonderful Whales

Pick up your pens, and finish these amazing
creatures with beautiful patterns.

Undersea Treats

The mermaids are having a feast.
Can you find these objects?

9 CORAL CUPCAKES

4 SHELL SPOONS

2 PARTY CROWNS

3 OCEAN LOLLIPOPS

Magical Land

Use your brightest pens and pencils
to bring this scene to life.

Starry Night

Shelly loves to swim to the surface at night, and gaze at the stars.
Can you spot this constellation?

Seadoku

Use the pictures above the grid to fill in the blank spaces.
You must arrange them so that each line across, each line down, and
each mini-grid has just one of each picture.

Code Queen

Ruby has left a coded message for Sparkle. Can you figure out what it says?

BRING   TO   SEA   CUPCAKES

LATER   BEACH   THE   THANKS

HELLO   PLEASE   FLOWER   PARTY

Butterfly Hunt

Eloise and her fairy friends are searching for the special blue butterfly with four wings. Can you help them find it?

Mermaid Song

Can you find a musical note that appears only once on this page?

Odd
Otter Out

Which of these sea otters
looks slightly different?

A

B

C

D

Perfect Presents

It's Rainbow's birthday! Can you unscramble the letters to figure out what all the other unicorns have bought her?

1 CIEOOKS

2 ERPFUEM

3 SRDSE

4 LOTHCES

5 UPKACCSE

Pet Puzzle

The unicorns have been exercising their pets, but their leashes have become tangled. Can you find out which pet belongs to which unicorn?

Mer-map

Use the grid on the map to answer the questions.
For example, the turtles are in square 2B.

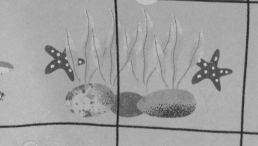

A

B

C

D

E

1 2 3 4 5

1. Look at square 4C. How many mermaids are there?

....

2. Find squares 5B, 5C, and 5D. Where is the octopus?

....

3. Is there a whale or a shark in 2E?

....

4. Which letter is on the row where the dolphins play?

....

5. Which square contains the Mer-king: 3A, 2E, or 4B?

....

6. What creature is in 3A?

....

7. If you want to visit the palace, should you go to 1B?

....

8. Which column has the most mermaids in it: 1, 3, or 4?

....

Flying Fair

There's a summer fair at the magical castle! Look at it for two minutes, then turn the page and answer the questions without going back.

Flying Fair

1. What is one of the fairies giving one of the unicorns?

....

2. Which ride is at the back of the fair?

....

3. Does the fairy looking in the mirror have blue or pink hair?

....

4. Is the fairy on the merry-go-round wearing a pink or purple dress?

....

5. Are the flags on the castle turrets red or yellow?

....

6. What instrument is one of the fairies playing?

....

Crab Course

Help Chloe the crab scuttle from start to finish by jumping on a pink shell, then a green one, then a purple one, repeating the pattern the whole way. She can only move downward and from side to side.

START

FINISH

Masterclass

Follow the step-by-step pictures to create your very own mermaid!

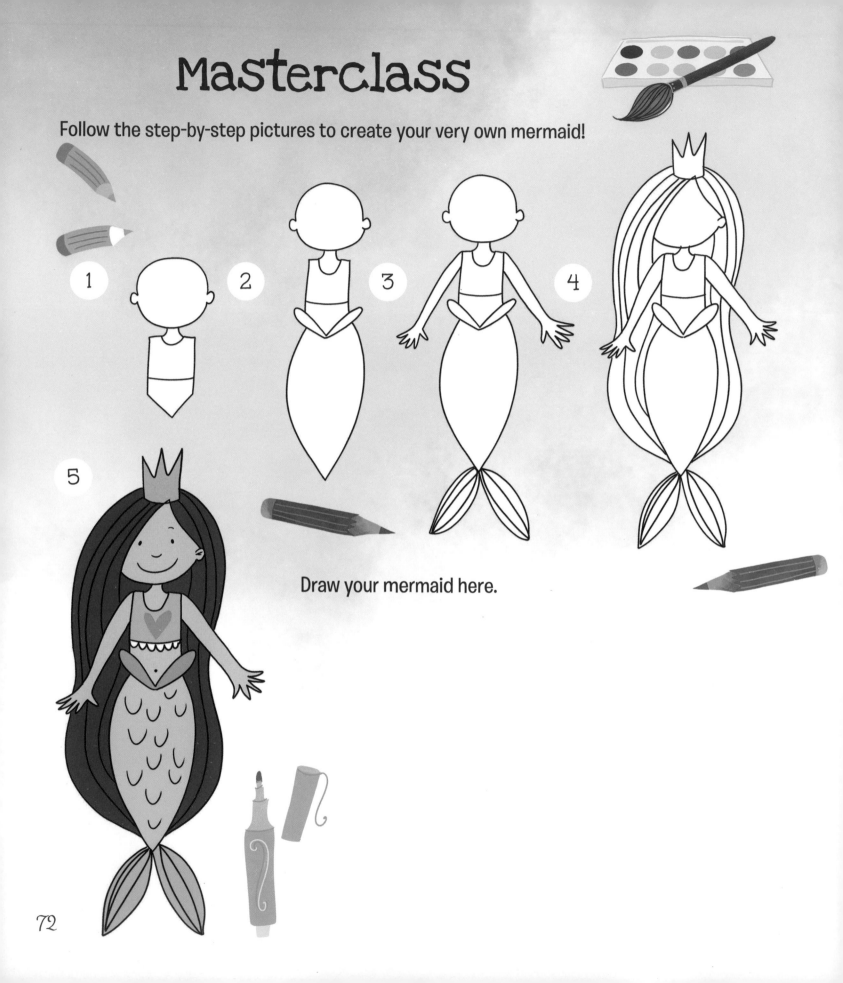

1

2

3

4

5

Draw your mermaid here.

Sky Visitors

The fantastic flying horses have arrived!
Can you spot the unicorn in this busy crowd?
After you've found her, use your pens and pencils
to decorate everyone.

Magical Unicorns

The mermaids love to leave the water to see what's happening on the land. Can you help the mermaids find Shimmer, their special unicorn friend? She has a purple horn and purple hooves.

Cool Creatures

Go wild with your pens and crayons to make
these creatures and plants even more amazing!

75

Party Perfect

These unicorns have dressed for a party in exactly the same outfits,
but one of them isn't dressed quite the same as the others.
Can you find who it is?

Cute Kites

These unicorns are kite-flying, but their strings are all in a tangle. Can you figure out which kite belongs to which?

Mermaid Whispers

It's so much fun playing games with your friends!
For this one, you'll need at least four of you, sitting in a line.

The person at one end (let's imagine it is you) thinks of something silly to say.
Try something like:

"Many of the mermaids get the giggles when they gossip."

Whisper it to the person sitting next to you. That person then whispers the message to the next person, but it has to be done immediately, with no thinking time, and you can only hear the message once.

Work to the end of the line, passing the message on quickly. There is a big chance that the message you end up with won't be anything like the original!

Tangled Tiaras

Oops! Aqua has got her tiaras in a big muddle.
Can you count how many there are on the page?

Flowery Trail

The Fairy Queen is lost in the garden! Can you help her find a way across? She has to step on the flowers in a set order. She can go up, down, left, and right, but not diagonally.

Start

Finish

80

Gorgeous Garlands

Primrose needs to pick the flower collection with the highest number of sparkle points, so she can make a special garland for her fairy friend, Lily. Which one should she choose?

Mirror, Mirror

These gorgeous mer-mirrors have all been found in the sand. They seem the same, but one of them is slightly different. Can you find it?

A

B

C

D

E

Wild Waves

Fill this page with waves, swirls, and pretty patterns, to remind you of the majestic ocean.

Super Sweet

Look carefully for these yummy treats!

CUPCAKE   CANDY   COOKIE   CHOCOLATE

DOUGHNUT   MANGO   CHERRY   LOLLIPOP

C	P	O	P	I	L	L	O	L	S
C	H	C	C	O	O	K	I	E	R
H	S	O	A	C	A	N	D	L	T
E	P	P	C	O	G	N	A	M	U
R	R	C	R	O	Y	L	C	H	N
R	I	H	R	D	L	O	A	Y	H
Y	B	R	N	L	T	A	N	R	G
I	E	A	L	L	O	Y	T	R	U
B	C	H	O	C	O	L	L	E	O
S	C	U	P	C	A	K	E	C	D

Home Time!

Can you help Sparklebreeze reach her castle?

Finish

Start

Find the Friends

The mermaids have lots of creatures to play with under the sea.
Look at the list, and then find all of them in the picture.

pink octopus

merboy

crab

clownfish

turtle

lobster

sea snail

blacktip shark

Forest Friends

Put this picture of Harvest and her woodland creatures back together! Can you spot which piece doesn't fit anywhere?

A
B
C
D
E
F
G

Beautiful Hair

Use your best pens to add long, magnificent manes and tails to these beautiful unicorns.
Let your imagination go wild, and add as many ribbons and bows as you like!

Splash!

Each of the dolphins has at least one identical friend, except one.
Can you find it?

Custom Made

Get creative with your pens and crayons to finish designing these beautiful accessories.

Knock! Knock!

It's getting dark, and Gumdrop can't remember the secret password to let her into the castle. Can you unscramble the letters, so she can get inside?

AFIYR

WIPSHRES

Fantasy Fairy Name

Your birth month + your fave sweet treat = your fairy name! For example, if you were born in May and liked strawberries, your name would be Violet Moon. Write down yours below!

JANUARY	POPPY	JULY	SILVER
FEBRUARY	WILLOW	AUGUST	SUGAR
MARCH	BLOSSOM	SEPTEMBER	BLUEBELL
APRIL	STAR	OCTOBER	HONEY
MAY	VIOLET	NOVEMBER	HARVEST
JUNE	IVY	DECEMBER	LILAC

CAKE	DAWN
COOKIES	BREEZE
STRAWBERRIES	MOON
ICE CREAM	GLOW
CHOCOLATE	SHINE
CANDY	SONG
POPCORN	GLIMMER
MILKSHAKE	DEWDROP

My fairy name is:

....

My friend's fairy name is:

....

Finders Keepers

Lots of pretty keys have sunk to the bottom of the ocean over the years!
Link each one to its pair, and find one that doesn't have a match.

Criss Cross

Which purse belongs to Shelly?
Join the dots in order to cross out all except one of them.

Festive Fun

It's Christmas, and Santa Claus has left presents! Can you find where all 11 of them are?

Awesome Ice

The unicorns are using their horns to make ice sculptures, but one sculpture has been made with a difference. Can you discover what it is?

Otter Spotter

Can you find this adorable baby otter in the crowd?

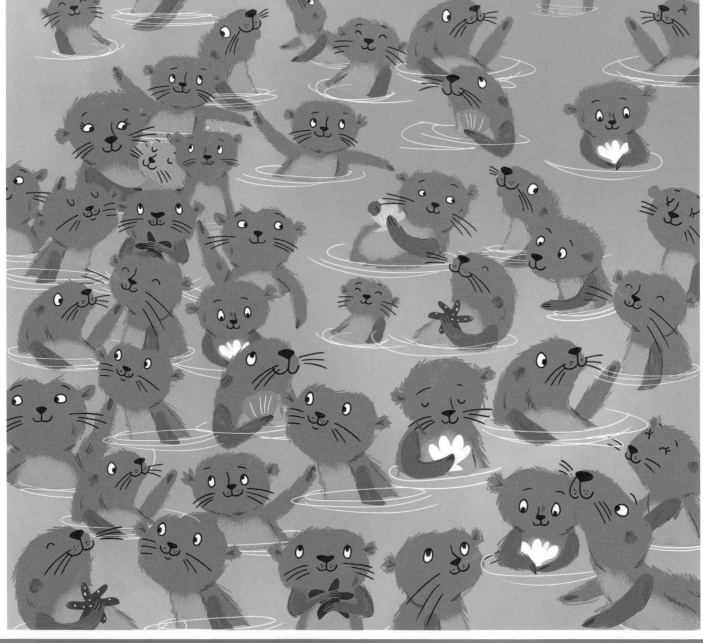

Super-search

Look for all the mermaids' magical friends hidden in this wordsearch grid. Words can be found forward, backward, and diagonally.

P	T	N	A	I	G	O	N
I	C	G	C	E	N	R	O
X	G	E	R	F	F	O	G
I	I	N	N	I	L	G	A
E	A	I	E	T	A	E	R
U	N	E	L	N	A	N	D
N	F	A	I	R	Y	U	N
U	N	I	C	O	R	N	R

FAIRY

PIXIE

ELF

GIANT

DRAGON

CENTAUR

UNICORN

GENIE

99

Tasty Treats!

There's a bake sale, and the fairies have made cakes and cookies. Can you find eight differences between these two yummy scenes?

Magical Mountain

The sugar fairies are flying over the swirly ice-cream mountains.
Can you figure out which one hasn't made the journey?

Sprinkle

Flossy

Buttercup

Lollipop

Cherry

Caramel

Sherbet

Ring, Ring!

Which of these beautiful gems does Shelly find in her treasure box?
Use the clues to work it out.

1. It contains at least one red stone.

2. It doesn't have any green stones on it.

3. It has three stones on it.

4. It contains at least one pink stone.

5. It doesn't have any blue stones.

Bubble Trouble

Find a way through the bubble maze to get to Casey the crab.

START

FINISH

Gem-tastic

Look carefully in the large grid to find this pattern of gems there.

Dressing Up

The mermaids are having a great time trying on each other's outfits!
Decorate them with your pens and crayons.

Paint the Rainbow

The unicorns have spotted a beautiful rainbow in the sky!
Use your best pens and pencils to bring it to life.

Castle Confusion

Which magical mermaid lives in which pretty sandcastle? Follow the water waves to find out!

Time for Bed

Can you spot six differences between these two pictures?

Twinkly Tiaras

Which two beautiful tiaras are exactly the same?

Rainbow Land

Can you put the pieces of this magical scene back together?
Which piece doesn't belong at all?

In the Treetops

The fairies are in the orchard collecting fruit.
Solve the equations to see which basket contains the most!

2

$14 + 8$

1

$36 - 7$

3

$16 + 9$

4

4×6

MAGICAL MUSIC

Melody is playing a beautiful tune for all of her friends.
Can you see which silhouette is exactly the same shape as the picture?

Pretty Patterns

Look along each line and work out what comes next to fill the spaces.

1

_____ _____

2

_____ _____

3

_____ _____

4

_____ _____

Fairy Picnic

Princess Poppy has made a list of all the things she wants at her birthday picnic.
Can you find all the words in the grid below?

GRAPES

JUICE

ICE CREAM

APPLES

SANDWICHES

LEMONADE

CAKE

MACARONS

I	I	C	E	C	R	E	A	M	A	S	S
G	L	E	M	O	N	A	D	E	A
R	R	C	S	K	L	E	M	H	A	N
E	G	R	A	N	M	C	A	K	E
C	C	R	S	A	I	A	P	P	W
I	H	S	A	W	P	N	P	A	I
U	O	A	D	P	R	P	E	K	C
J	C	N	R	D	E	R	L	D	H
C	A	E	P	R	M	S	S	E	E
S	S	N	N	R	A	C	A	M	S

Mermaid Rock

Bring this magical sea scene to life!

Quiz Time

Which of the mermaids would you have as your BFF?
Answer the questions and keep count of the letters you pick as you go along.

1. Do you prefer clothes in shades of?

A. Pink.

B. Purple.

C. Blue.

D. Yellow.

2. Which of these do you enjoy the most?

A. Chatting.

B. Reading.

C. TV.

D. Drawing.

3. What creature would you like as a pet?

A. A dog or a cat.

B. A mouse or a fish.

C. A tortoise or a lizard.

D. A gerbil or a hamster.

4. What would your friends say is the best thing about you?

A. You are funny.

B. You are kind.

C. You are generous.

D. You are smart.

5. How do you wear your hair at the weekend?

A. Clipped away from your eyes.

B. In a bun.

C. Loose and flowing.

D. All ways–weekends are for experimenting!

6. What kind of job would you like when you're grown up?

A. Working with animals.

B. Something creative.

C. Working with people.

D. Something brainy.

7. Who knows more of your secrets than anyone?

A. Your mother.

B. Your best friend.

C. Your father.

D. Only your diary knows ...

Results

Mostly As

You and Coral would get along swimmingly! She loves exciting things—parties, music, fashion—the brighter and bolder the better! You are probably one of the first in your group to get noticed, but that's fine by you!

Mostly Bs

Shelly is your shoal-mate! You both love to be in a crowd, and are happiest when you're surrounded by friends and family. The only things that really make you sad are being lonely, or others being unkind.

Mostly Cs

You're like Aqua—calm, sweet, and gentle. She is always willing to lend a helping hand, and that is one of your best qualities, too. We hope your friends appreciate what a lovely person you are!

Mostly Ds

Hey, Pearl-friend! You and this mermaid have so much in common—clever and creative, you would be happy curled up together in a corner with a book or a sketchpad.

119

Stunning Sandcastle

Can you decorate the mermaids' home with drawings of pretty shells and sea creatures?

120

Shadow Me

Which of these silhouettes is an exact match for Shelley and her pet sea horse, Snorkley?

Shell Seeker

Can you find a shell that looks like this, somewhere in the sand?

122

Fishy Friends

Copy these happy fish, then decorate them with your pens or pencils.

Birthday Surprises

What has each mermaid been bought for her birthday?
Unscramble the letters to find out!

1. NCE CEKLA

2. AIRH BRUHS

3. SPR EAL

4. MOR RIR

5. HRM CAS

Draw Me!

Follow the steps to create this magical mermaid.

Celebrations

Which of these birthday cakes does Aqua want for her party?
Use the clue to find out!

1. It isn't heart-shaped.

2. It doesn't have any rainbow sprinkles.

3. It is decorated with starfish.

4. It has shells on top.

A

B

C

D

E

Party time

Can you find the three framed sections, somewhere in the party scene?

1

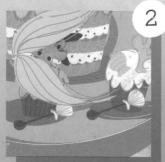

2

3

127

Magical Mix-Up

The unicorns and fairies have been to the fair, and have each won a balloon, but their strings are in a tangle. Can you see which balloon belongs to which pair?

Make a Splash!

The mermaids are playing water volleyball, while the unicorns and fairies cheer them on.
Can you fit the circles into the scene? Which of the circles cannot be placed?

A   B   C   D   E   F   G

Unique Fish

Which butterflyfish doesn't have a twin?

Remember, Remember

Take a good look at this scene, remembering as much as you can.
Then turn the page and test your memory!

Remember, Remember

Can you remember what you saw? Write down
everything you can!

1. Which animal was in the tree?

....

2. How many mermaids were swimming?

....

3. Which two of these butterflies did you see?

A B C

4. Which creature is sitting on a mermaid's lap?

....

5. What do the toadstools look like?

A B C

6. Who is flying in the sky?

....

7. Which of these mermaids has her hands in her hair?

A B C

8. Are the rabbits white or brown?

....

Treasure Trove

Can you find all the precious things that Pearl stores in her chest? Words can be found forward, backward, and diagonally.

PEARL

DIAMOND

OPAL

RUBY

R	D	I	P	E	N	G	W
U	N	A	E	E	N	R	C
B	O	E	A	I	A	W	R
E	M	E	R	A	L	D	O
M	A	N	L	U	A	E	W
T	I	A	R	A	B	A	N
R	D	I	L	S	B	Y	R
E	E	R	E	L	A	P	O

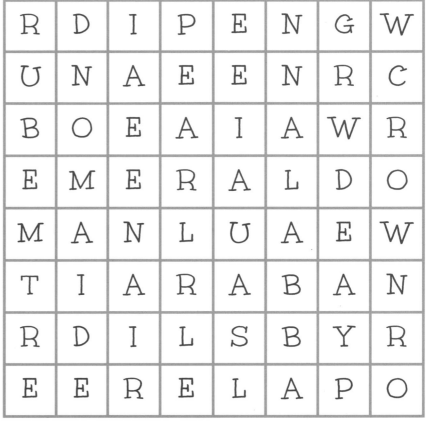

RING

TIARA

CROWN

EMERALD

133

Delicious Desserts

Look at this picture of the fairy kitchen for two minutes.
Then turn the page, and answer the questions without looking back.

Delicious Desserts

1. What is the fairy bringing out of the oven?

....

2. Is the yellow fairy wearing a crown or a rose?

....

3. Is the unicorn's apron blue or pink?

....

4. Does the tablecloth have hearts or stars on it?

....

5. How many cups are on the table?

....

6. Which fruit are the fairies using to decorate the cake?

....

Flashing Fireflies

The unicorns are watching the pretty fireflies in the sky. Can you tell which one looks a little bit different?

In the Clouds

Loveheart needs to find a way across the cloud kingdom to join the fairies. Can you help her cross, following the order?

1

2

3

Start

Finish

Dainty Dewdrops

The raindrop fairies are off to collect water from the dew waterfall. Can you guide them through the tropical forest to reach it?

Start

Finish

139

Find the Flowers

There are so many beautiful flowers in the unicorns' magical land. Can you find all of their names hidden in the grid?

ROSE · LILY · SUNFLOWER · LILAC

IRIS · DAISY · TULIP · ORCHID

L	U	N	F	L	O	L	I	S	Y
I	T	U	L	I	P	U	L	I	O
C	R	O	D	P	L	I	Y	T	R
A	R	E	C	A	U	N	O	R	C
L	D	S	I	S	I	R	I	A	H
I	L	O	L	T	I	S	N	R	I
L	T	R	O	P	Y	D	Y	F	D
S	U	N	F	L	O	W	E	R	L
O	W	E	I	I	S	U	N	L	H
R	O	L	A	F	E	L	D	A	C

Pretty Patterns

Decorate the horns, heads, and necks of these unicorns with swirls and stars!

Giddy Up!

Coral is having a great time riding her special sea horse.
Which of the silhouette outlines matches the main picture?

Watch Out!

Can you find six sneaky sharks hiding in this scene?

Pretty Ribbons

Violet can't find her special bow. Can you help her?
It's the only one that doesn't have an exact match,
and she's not already wearing it.

144

Diving Deep

Add some magic to this underwater scene.

Get Creative!

What has happened here? Write a story based on the pictures. It can be whatever you want, so use your imagination!

Say Hello!

Unscramble the letters to find out the names of these four friendly mermaids.

ORCAL

AREPL

B

A

HYLELS

QAUA

C

D

Deck the Halls!

The unicorns and fairies are decorating the Christmas tree. Can you find eight differences between these two festive scenes?

Castle Games

The unicorns have hidden themselves all over the magical castle. Can you find all ten of them?

Scaredy Fish

Something has frightened poor Bubbles the puffer fish!
See if you can spot eight difference between the two pictures.

Pattern Mad

Copy this picture of the friendly whale, and then decorate it with your pens or pencils.

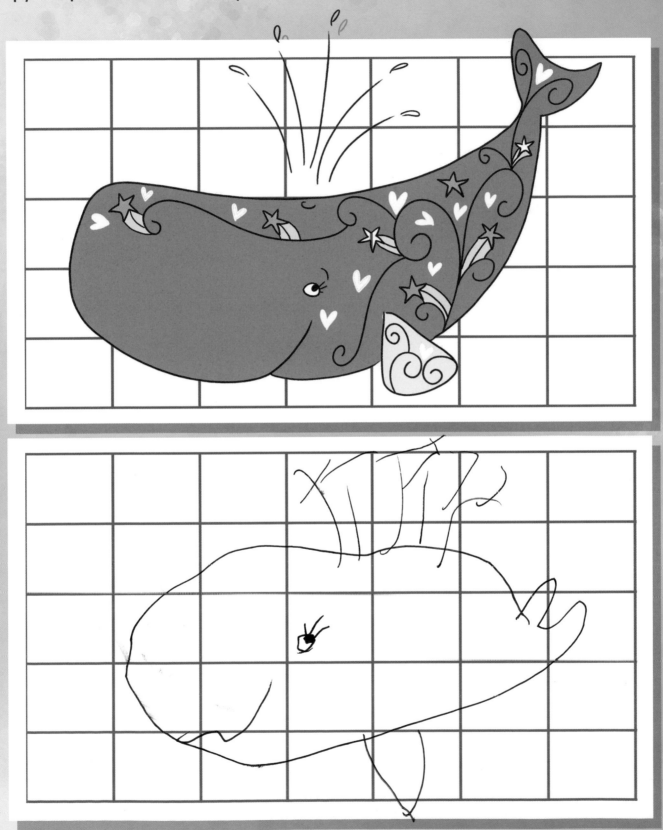

Magical Mermaid Name

The shell you think is the prettiest + the fish you think looks the friendliest = your mermaid name. For example, if you liked both the first shell and the first fish on the left, your name would be Coral Star.

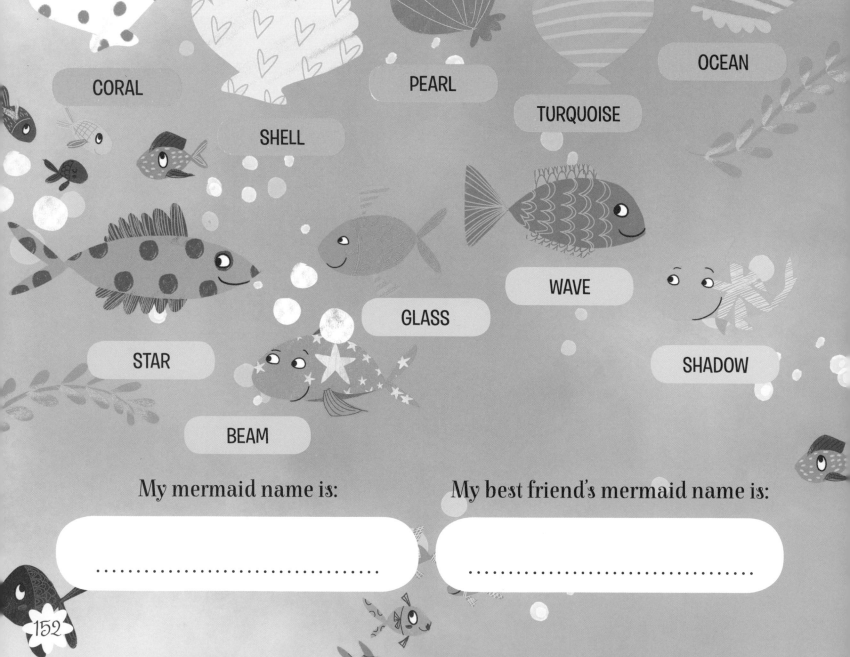

CORAL

PEARL

OCEAN

TURQUOISE

SHELL

WAVE

GLASS

STAR

SHADOW

BEAM

My mermaid name is:

....

My best friend's mermaid name is:

....

152

Snug Knitwear

It's getting chilly, so the fairies have been making hats and scarves for the unicorns. However, the sparkle threads are in a tangle. Can you figure out which fairy has knitted which item?

1

2

3

4

A

B

C

D

Fluttering Fairies

Draw these cute fairy friends by copying them into the grid below!

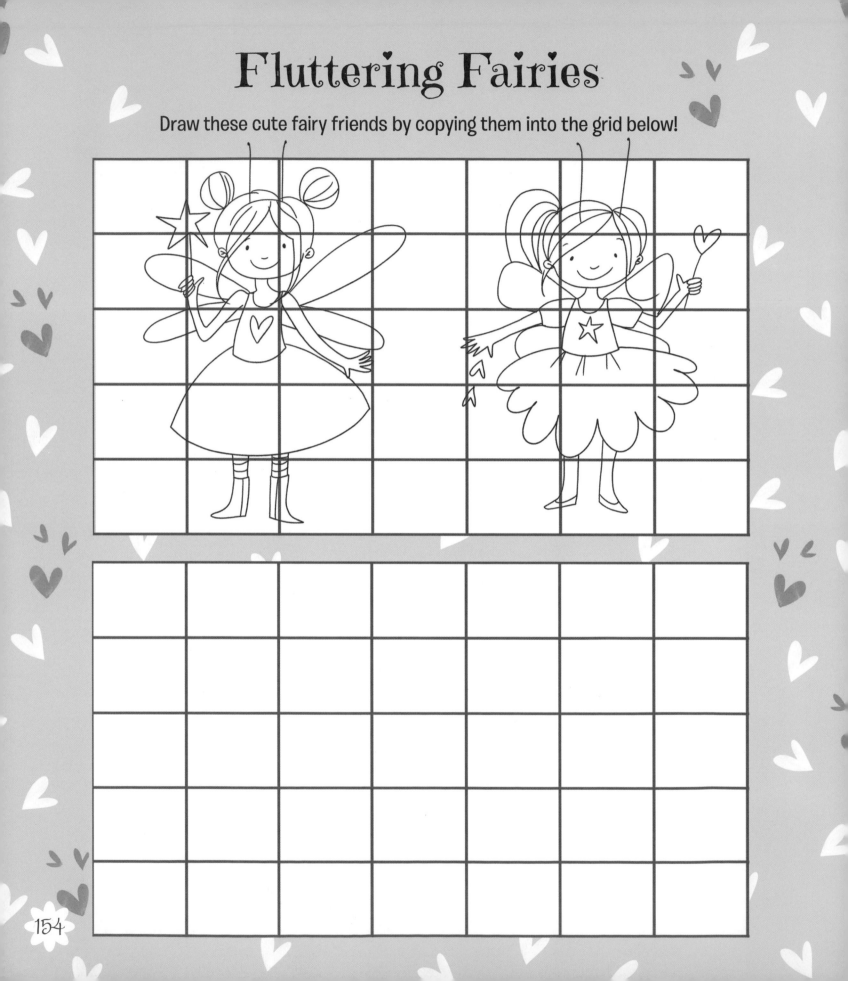

Friends Forever

Invent cute names for all of these fairy pairs,
then write them in the boxes below!

. . . .

. . . .

. . . .

. . . .

. . . .

. . . .

. . . .

. . . .

. . . .

. . . .

. . . .

. . . .

155

Magical Feast

The unicorns are having a magical meal!
Can you work out what they're serving for each course?

Starter

SKERAPE IEP

....

Main course

**CHCOÀTLOE
BREINWOS**

....

....

Dessert

**WELTREMOAN
ELIHGDT**

....

....

Precious Pet

Sparkle can't find her pet kitten, Cloudpuff!
Can you see where she is hiding?

Cute Shell-fie!

These BFFs have printed shell-fies!
Which one of them is a tiny bit different from the others?

Looking Out

What can Shelly see from her window? You decide, then add it to the picture and complete it with pens and pencils.

159

Leaping High

Which unicorn is the best at rainbow jumping?
Calculate who has the highest score to find out!

1

1/2 of 28

2

30 - 15

3

3 x 6

4

36 ÷ 4

Pearl's Purse

Where has Pearl left her purse?
See if you can find it for her.

Answers

Page 3: Come On In!
Pathway B leads to the castle.

Page 4: Twin Teaser

Page 5: Time for Tea!

Page 6: Under the Sea

Page 7: Beautiful Babies
1 A, 2 C, 3 B

Page 8: Party Prep

Page 9: #selfie

Page 10: Gift Giving
A, A

Page 12: Super Starfish

Answers

Page 13: Friendly Fish

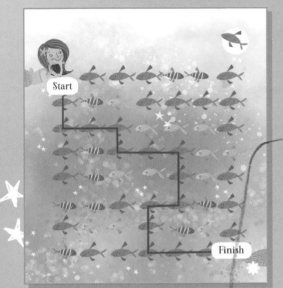

Page 16: Find Me!

Page 18: Bobbing Along

Page 15: Stormy Seas

Page 17: Best Fairy Friends

Page 19: Secret Message

JOIN OUR FUN

Page 21: Which Way?

Answers

Pages 22-23: Seeing Stars
28

Page 24: Winged Wonders
Butterflies: Twelve, Fairies: Nine.
There are more butterflies.

Page 25: Magical Trail

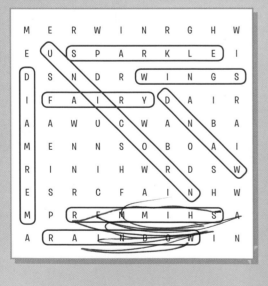

Page 26: Round and Round
Squirt

Page 27: Coco the Clown

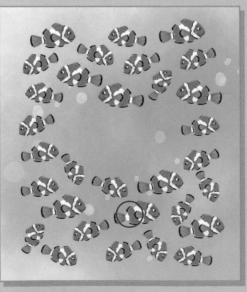

Page 28: Pool Party

Page 30: Magical Mer-king
D

Page 31: Undersea Creatures

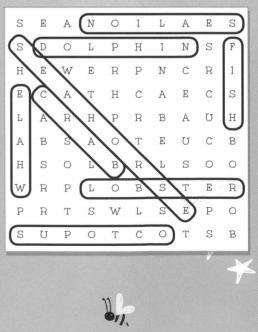

Answers

Page 32: Shiny Crown

Pages 34-35: Golden Bells and Pearl Shells

Golden bells: 7. Pearl shells: 14.

Page 33: Cloud Kingdom

Page 36: Beautiful Bows

1 D
2 B
3 C
4 A

Page 37: Pearl Problem

Page 38: Wavy Hair!

C

Page 39: Mer-maze

165

Answers

Page 41: Queen of the Arts

Page 44: Lost Jewels

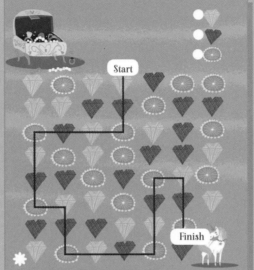

Page 48: Shining Bright

Page 42: Shell Sorting

11

9

8

8

4

Page 46: Magical Memories

1 A balloon.
2 She's wearing a hat.
3 There are four fairies.
4 Two unicorns.
5 Four mermaids.
6 A snail.

Page 47: Missing Link
Lobster

Page 49: Find the Fairy

Page 50: Lost and Found
C

Answers

Page 51: Watery Words

Some of the words you could have found were:

ADD

AID

DEN

HEARD

HIDE

RUST

SHUT

SIDE

SURE

STAND

THERE

THREE

TURN

Page 53: Adorable Outfits

Page 56: Undersea Treats

Page 58: Starry Night

Page 59: Seadoku

Page 60: Code Queen

The message is:
Please bring cupcakes to the
beach party later.

Page 61: Butterfly Hunt

Answers

Page 62: Mermaid Song

Page 63: Odd Otter Out

C - the tail is curling a different way.

Page 64: Perfect Presents

1 Cookies
2 Perfume
3 Dress
4 Clothes
5 Cupcakes

Page 65: Pet Puzzle

1 D
2 C
3 A
4 B

Pages 66–67: Mer-map

1 2
2 5C
3 A whale
4 A
5 4B
6 A whale
7 No, 4B and 5B
8 Column 1

Page 70: Flying Fair

1 A medal.
2 The ferris wheel.
3 She has pink hair.
4 She is wearing a purple dress.
5 The flags are yellow.
6 The fairy is playing a harp.

Page 71: Crab Course

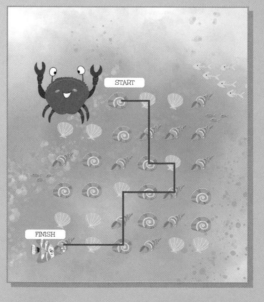

Page 73: Sky Visitors

Page 74: Magical Unicorns

Answers

Page 76: Party Perfect

Page 77: Cute Kites

1 C
2 D
3 A
4 B

Page 79: Tangled Tiaras

12

Page 80: Flowery Trail

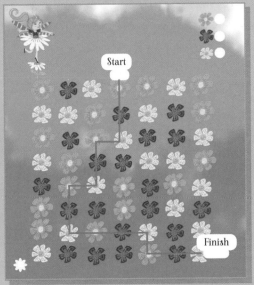

Page 81: Gorgeous Garlands

Pile A has the most.

A has 19.
B has 11.
C has 17.
D has 18.

Page 82: Mirror, Mirror

C

Page 84: Super Sweet

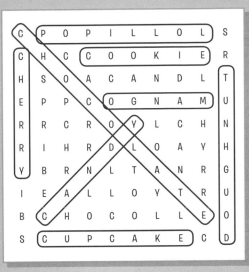

Page 85: Home Time!

169

Answers

Pages 86–87: Find the Friends

Page 88: Forest Friends

Piece D doesn't fit anywhere.

Page 90: Splash!

Page 92: Knock! Knock!

The secret password is:
Fairy Whispers.

Page 94: Finders Keepers

Page 95: Criss Cross

D

Answers

Page 96: Festive Fun

Page 97: Awesome Ice

Page 98: Otter Spotter

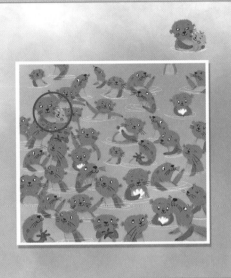

Page 99: Super-search

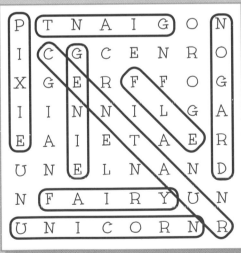

Page 100: Tasty Treats!

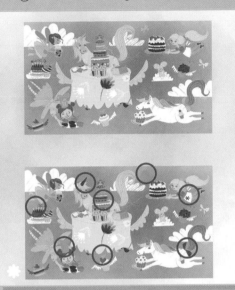

Page 101: Magical Mountain

Cherry hasn't made the journey.

Page 102: Ring, Ring!

D

Page 103: Bubble Trouble

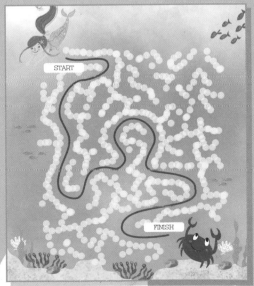

Answers

Page 104–105: Sparkling Snow

Page 106: Gem-tastic

Page 109
Castle Confusion

1 C
2 B
3 D
4 A

Page 110: Time for Bed

Page 111: Twinkly Tiaras

Page 112: Rainbow Land

Piece A does not belong.

Answers

Page 113: In the Treetops

Page 116: Fairy Picnic

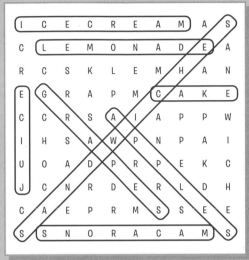

Page 122: Shell Seeker

Page 114: Magical Music

B

Page 115: Pretty Patterns

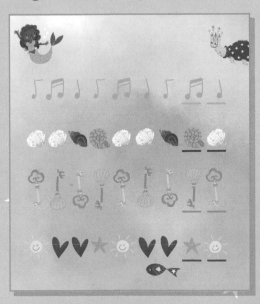

Page 121: Shadow Me

Page 124:
Birthday Surprises

1 Necklace   4 Mirror
2 Hairbrush   5 Charms
3 Pearls

Page 126: Celebrations

C

Answers

Page 127: Party Time

Page 128: Magical Mix-Up

1 D
2 B
3 C
4 A

Page 129: Make a Splash!

Circle C cannot be placed.

Page 130: Unique Fish

Page 132: Remember, Remember

1 Squirrels
2 2
3 A, C
4 A bird
5 A
6 Fairies
7 C
8 White

Page 133: Treasure Trove

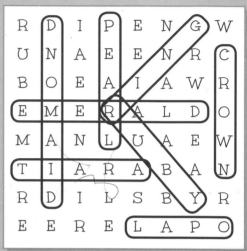

Page 136: Delicious Desserts

1 Cookies.
2 The yellow fairy is wearing a crown.
3 The unicorn's apron is blue.
4 Stars.
5 There are three cups on the table.
6 Strawberries.

Page 137: Flashing Fireflies

Answers

Page 138: In the Clouds

Page 139: Dainty Dewdrops

Page 140: Find the Flowers

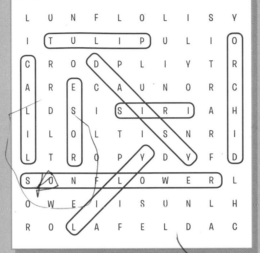

L	U	N	F	L	O	L	I	S	Y
I	T	U	L	I	P	U	L	I	O
C	R	O	D	P	L	I	Y	T	R
A	R	E	C	A	U	N	O	R	C
L	D	S	I	S	I	R	I	A	H
I	L	O	L	T	I	S	N	R	I
L	T	R	O	P	Y	D	Y	F	D
S	O	N	F	L	O	W	E	R	L
O	W	E	I	I	S	U	N	L	H
R	O	L	A	F	E	L	D	A	C

Page 142: Giddy Up!

D

Page 143: Watch Out!

Page 144: Pretty Ribbons

Page 147: Say Hello!

A Coral, B Pearl, C Aqua, D Shelly

Page 148: Deck the Halls!

175

Answers

Page 149: Castle Games

Page 150: Scaredy Fish

Page 153: Snug Knitwear

1 D
2 C
3 A
4 B

Page 156: Magical Feast

Starter: Sparkle pie

Main course: Chocolate brownies

Dessert: Watermelon delight

Page 157: Precious Pet

Page 158: Cute Shell-fie!

Page 160: Leaping High

Number 3 is the best at rainbow jumping.

Page 161: Pearl's Purse